BOXERS

Marcel Nijland

BOXERS

REBO
PUBLISHERS

© 2004 Zuid Boekprodukties
© 2006 Rebo Publishers

Text: Marcel Nijland
Cover design and layout: AdAm Studio, Prague, The Czech Republic
Typesetting and pre-press services: A. R. Garamond, Prague,
The Czech Republic
Translation: Guy Shipton for First Edition Translations Ltd, Cambridge, UK
Editing: David Price for First Edition Translations Ltd, Cambridge, UK
Proofreading: Sarah Dunham

ISBN 13: 978-90-366-1086-5
ISBN 10: 90-366-1086-9

CONTENTS

Boxers still have
something of the
former
Bullenbeisser
about them

1 HISTORY

Earliest history

Within the dog family, the boxer belongs among the group known as mastiffs. The oldest remains of mastiff-like dogs date from approximately five thousand years ago, placing mastiffs among the oldest of the world's dog breeds. Mastiffs were bred early on for a specific purpose, which usually involved guarding duties and hunting large game. The Assyrians and Romans also deployed them as dogs of war. The boxer's early ancestors were the large fighting dogs with which the Assyrians and Romans went into battle. These Assyrian mastiffs were the ancestors of the English mastiff, the French mastiff (dogue de Bordeaux), the Italian Neapolitan mastiff, and the Swiss Bernese mountain dog and Saint Bernard. These venerable breeds of mastiff spread out across Europe with new breeds developing from them in many countries. Belgium produced the Matin, Denmark the Broholmer, and Italy, in addition to the Neapolitan mastiff, the Cane Corso. The large mastiff-like mountain dogs that protect herds of cattle against wild animals also descend from the same forebears.

A boxer circa 1900

Bullenbeissers

Ordinary people could not afford these huge mastiffs and, moreover, they needed dogs that were more versatile. Large mastiffs were crossed with faster, nimbler dogs to make them more suitable for bull baiting-in German Bullenbeisser dogs, literally "bull biters." These small, nimble mastiffs would fight with a bull, attempting to keep the bull in check by grasping its nose and gripping tightly onto it. At first, this was done because people believed it improved the flavor of the beef. However, it soon gave rise to a form of public entertainment on which bets were placed. This barbaric "sport," which took place in a great many European countries, required lightweight, agile dogs that, nevertheless, were strong enough to enter the fray. Bull baiting was banned in the first half of the nineteenth century. Subsequently, in Germany, a modern breed came

Tenacity

to be bred from the old Danzig and Brabanter bullenbeisser breeds – the boxer.

The modern boxer: a mixture of different breeds

The Danzig bullenbeisser was a fairly heavy mastiff; the Brabanter bullenbeisser was somewhat lighter and more agile. It was probably the latter that left the greatest mark on the present-day boxer. The nineteenth-century English bulldog, lighter footed and with a less extreme body frame than its modern counterpart, also played a role in this genetic inheritance.

The nineteenth century

The 1880s saw the appearance of two animals that are now viewed as the progenitors of the modern boxer: Tom and Flora. Flora had been brought from France by one Georg Alt, who lived in Munich, Germany. Alt's Flora was mated locally with a similar type of dog. Flora's male offspring, named "Lechner's box" after his owner, is considered to be the first boxer dog. Tom was an English bulldog and a prominent stud dog in this preliminary period. According to his description, he was an athletic dog and "as white as snow." It is suspected that the many white boxers that continue to be born even to

The modern boxer is more elegant than its predecessors of a century ago

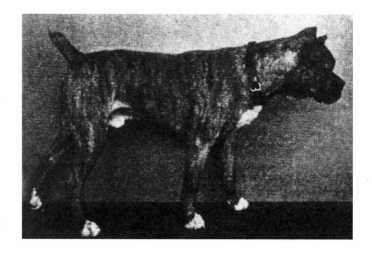

this day are descendants of "Snow-White Tom." Tom was pair-ed with one of Flora's granddaughters and from this pairing came the first boxer to be exhibited at a show: Flocki. An exa-mination of pictures from the past shows that it was only by the 1930s that boxers lost the "bull terrier head" and truly came to resemble the modern boxer we recognize today. It was also during this period that the breed made a break-through in England, and in the Netherlands and Germany boxer clubs were founded; these were devoted entirely to esta-blishing and promoting a breed standard.

The boxer arrived in the United States in 1903, and the breed was first registered by the A.K.C. in 1904, well before there was a national parent club. The American public first became aware of the boxer in 1912, thanks to the importation of a des-cendant of Flocki, Dampf von Dom, by the future governor of New York, Herbert H. Lehman. In 1915, Dampf became the first boxer to receive championship honors in the United States. The American Boxer Club was founded in 1935, and the club became a member of the A.K.C. in May 1936.

The name

It is not entirely clear where the English-sounding name "boxer" origina-ted from. Possibly, it is a corruption of an earlier name: "boxl."
However, it may simply be that the name refers to the dog's tendency to use its forelegs like a boxer when playing or fighting.

2 THE BREED STANDARD

Origins of the breed standard

The kennel club in the country of origin draws up a breed standard for each officially recognized breed. The breed standard describes the appearance of an ideal representative of a given breed and animals are judged at shows on the basis of that standard. Germany was the first to draw up a breed standard for boxers. Nowadays, our perception of the ideal image is undergoing some change and it has been shown in some breeds that certain requirements of the standard can damage the animals' health. Consequently, breed standards are amended from time to time. Of course, each country has its own approach. The breed standard is a written document that can leave room open for individual interpretation. The standard is not usually so detailed as to prevent judges from being able to make any distinction between animals. With regard to boxers, for example, there was for many years a trend that favored extremely truncated noses. However, this truncation hampered respiration to such an extent that it limited proper work performance and athletic capability. At present, the aim is for a more balanced relationship between skull length and nose muzzle length. This puts the boxer

The shape of the head has undergone some significant changes in the past

Wrinkles on the forehead are permitted but should not cause turned out eyelids

back in its rightful place as a sports dog and athlete (as in the past).

A.K.C.
The American Kennel Club (A.K.C.) is an umbrella organization that coordinates clubs and pure breeding across the United States.
Other kennel clubs exist across the world, of course, such as the Canadian Kennel Club and European Kennel Club (F.C.I.). Different kennel clubs sometimes employ slightly different breed standards.

The breed standard

General appearance: a boxer is a medium-sized, square-built dog with strong limbs and a powerful, well-developed musculature.

Behavior and character: boxers must look self-confident and be composed and even-tempered. They have long been renowned for the devotion and loyalty they show to their keeper and the keeper's whole family, as well as for their alertness and their unflinching courage as guard dogs. They present no danger to family members, but are suspicious of strangers; they are lively and amiable when playing, but fearless when matters become serious.

Head: without too many wrinkles and with a full muzzle two-thirds the width of the skull. The dark mask does not extend beyond the muzzle. The forehead shows an indentation between the eyes, although this should not be too pronounced, and creates a distinct stop where the forehead meets the topline of the muzzle.

Nose: broad and black, slightly turned up, wide nostrils with a groove between them. The tip of the nose should lie slightly higher than the root of the muzzle.

Eyes: as dark as possible and encircled by dark hair. Should not be too small, too protruding, or too deep set.

A brindle-colored male dog

Bite: the lower jaw protrudes beyond the upper jaw and has a slight upward curvature. A boxer's bite is undershot.

Neck: strong, muscular, without wrinkles, or dewlaps.

Ears: set high at highest point of the skull. When not cropped, small rather than large ears, falling forward with a definite crease.

Body: square build. The body is supported by sturdy, straight limbs.

Hindquarters: strongly muscled, clearly visible beneath the skin.

Tail: the tail is set high, docked, and carried upward.

Feet: small with compact, well-arched toes (cat feet) and tough pads.

Coat: short, glossy, and lying smooth and tight against the body.

Color: fawn or brindle. Fawn ranges in various shades from light tan to stag red or mahogany. Brindle varies from a fawn background with dark stripes to a dark background with fawn stripes. The background color and stripes may not intermingle to such an extent that the stripes lose their definition. White patches may not account for more than one third of the background color.

Height at withers: dogs, 22.5 to 25 inches (57 to 63 cm); bitches 21 to 23.5 inches (53 to 59 cm).

Weight: dogs 77 to 86 lbs (35 to 39 kg); bitches 62 to 70.5 lbs (28 to 32 kg).

Breeding policy

It is worth emphasizing that the breed standard says little about faults and any abnormalities. Breeders' associations bridge these gaps in a breed standard by developing a breeding policy that pays particular attention to medical matters.

An attempt is thus made to breed healthy boxers by investigating family trees, checking for abnormalities, such as hip dysplasia (HD), and taking other measures besides.

This breeding policy also includes measures aimed at countering excesses within the dog breeding community. For example, an association will usually act as an agent only for a limited number of litters per bitch in order to prevent the bitch from being serviced on every occasion that she comes into season. This policy aims to stop an individual dog from becoming a victim of her owner's ambition or desire for financial gain.

3 CHARACTER

A family dog

Boxers are family dogs beyond comparison. Their curiosity and perkiness mean their short noses get stuck into everything. Family business is their business too. By nature boxers are very active dogs, but without being nervy or demanding. They adore playing and romping about, and are not easily affected by less pleasant experiences. This stability of character makes them ideal family dogs.

They are not difficult to train either. Boxers can perform most impressively, particularly when using modern training methods, where the reward system plays a pivotal role.

A bundle of energy

As mentioned previously, a boxer is an extremely active dog that must be allowed to release its energy. Whether you walk or cycle, long daily excursions with a boxer are essential. A little mental training also does the animal good. Obedience training can be taught to a high level, and being given additional challenges is extremely important to this breed. This does not

Boxers make an excellent choice for children because of their amiable character

always have to be done through a local club. Searching for a ball, learning tricks, or playing with other dogs all fulfill this need, just as long as they can be kept fully occupied for a while. The energetic trait of boxers is particularly evident in pups and young dogs. Tirelessly, they nose forward their toys to challenge you to a game. Dogs of about a year old can tire out their owners with their unbridled energy. Therefore be forewarned that a year-old dog makes his presence emphatically known, even if you have already come a long way in training him. Boxers want active owners who take the initiative in doing things together.

A one-man dog?

In guidebooks dating back a few years, boxers were frequently portrayed as typical "one-man" dogs: in other words, dogs that bond expressly with one member of the family. It is open to question how far this is in fact true. Most dogs often seem to bond rather more with one person in a family compared with the other family members. Boxers are no exception. Nevertheless, it is not correct to characterize boxers as typical one-man (or one-woman) dogs. Their character is too open and sociable for this, and they are too keen to be at the center of the action, whomever it may involve and wherever it is. Boxers are true family dogs that can well tolerate a fair crowd of people.

Child-friendly

Boxers are renowned for their friendliness with children and this is certainly true. Once properly trained, boxers are dogs that seldom mean mischief and put up well with the odd knock or shove. They have a reasonably high pain threshold, and tend not to be so quick to react with anxiety or aggression when handled a little roughly by a child. However, this should come with a warning attached: in the heat of the moment their enthusiasm can overspill and, generally speaking, they are less inclined to withdraw from commotion but, rather, like to take an active part in it. This means that you must always supervise any play with children. Teach boxers to treat small children with care. It is better for you to prohibit any horsing about with the dog unless the child does so extremely carefully. Older children (older than ten) are better able to hold their own against a dog's strength and speed. However, a boxer is often just a little too strong and boisterous even for children in that age group, making it difficult for them to keep the dog under control.

Not too rough

If children often handle a dog roughly, this may result in the dog learning to anticipate that treatment. This may cause the dog to adopt defensive

behavior. It is for that reason that rough play should be avoided at all times so that if it does get a little too rough on one occasion, the dog will be less likely to react to it with undesirable behavior.

A boxer will make a point of guarding your property

Differences between dogs and bitches

The differences between dogs and bitches can be observed in every breed of dog. However, the golden rule with all mammals is that males get involved in more serious fights, and more frequently, about things such as food, breeding, and rank.

Boxers are no exception to this. Male dogs are slightly more difficult to train and are more likely to assert themselves than bitches. Hormonal influences are largely responsible for this behavior and any training has to take this into account.

4 PURCHASE

Preparation

Before getting yourself a boxer, you are recommended to meet and observe a few boxers in your neighborhood. Shows provide good opportunities for this as well. Breeders can usually be found among the participants, or there will be other enthusiasts who will be able to put you on the right track information-wise within the boxer dog fraternity. Find out everything you can from breed enthusiasts. Try to find out whether the image they paint about the breed coincides with what you have seen. Of course, all enthusiasts feel that their breed is adorable, faithful, and has many more positive characteristics besides. In this orientation phase, pay close attention above all to whether the breed's temperament suits you. A show ring provides another opportunity for observation, where differences between breeds become obvious.

You can also build a bond with an older dog

Should I get a pup ...?

If you have decided to purchase a boxer, the next question is whether to get a pup or an adult dog. Many are tempted to choose a pup, on the assumption that a pup can be brought completely under their control. Pups do indeed make excellent candidates for training. However, training a pup is quite a serious undertaking, involving you in a year of intensive work at the least. Furthermore, things can sometimes go slightly awry during training, resulting in you emerging from the battle with a dog rather different than your envisaged ideal. In other words, you cannot necessarily say how a young pup's character is going to develop.

... or an adult dog?

For whatever reason, some people are forced to part with a dog that they have cherished. The dog then ends up in an animal shelter, or is offered for sale through a breeders' association, or else in an advertisement in a newspaper or on the Internet. Under certain circumstances, such an adult dog does have points in its favor. If, immediately after purchase, you are regularly away from home for a while, it is easier to get started with an adult dog than it would be with pups, because they demand less attention. In other words, an older dog does not normally need any more obedience lessons or housetraining. Naturally enough, this applies only to dogs that have been well cared for and have had time and effort spent on them. It is also easier to tell from an older dog than it is from a pup exactly what you are getting for your money.

Sometimes an older dog is a great choice too

For example, physical abnormalities can more easily be spotted once an animal is fully grown. Thus there can be distinct advantages in looking at adult boxers as well as pups. The bond that you can build with the animal will be no less strong than that with a dog raised in your home since a pup.

The breeder
Finding a good breeder is best done through people who are well-known among the boxer fraternity. Word-of-mouth advertising is usually the best recommendation that a breeder can hope for. Additionally, the breeders' association (or kennel club) can give you the names and addresses of bree-

A healthy young boxer is a barrelful of energy

*They can become
excellent pals with
other dogs*

ders registered with the association, which mean that they comply with the quality standards set by the club. Of course, you should make a thorough study of what the association's standards actually involve. The standards that a breeders' association can impose on breeders, if they wish to be considered for trading pups, would have to include the following:
• Checks on the parent animals for hereditary faults
• Plenty of space in which pups can be raised responsibly
• Limited number of litters per annum

Signs of a good breeder
• The pups are clean and have been brought up with plenty of space to run around
• The pups look healthy (clean eyes, clean anus, glossy coat)
• The pups come into frequent contact with people (adults and children)
• Good breeders make a point of meeting and getting to know you
• The breeder is able to show you the results of the medical examination

---

Look out for abnormalities

There are a number of boxer abnormalities that you should be familiar with before purchasing a pup. Boxers have very short noses, which can often result in noisy breathing. They are athletic and lively as a breed, and respiratory problems are a hindrance to this. Constricted breathing damages the well-being of the animal and the breed standard. This is something that you must go out of your way to check when purchasing a pup. See whether its nostrils are open and whether it can breathe freely without any background noise. Sniffling and snorting indicate that the nasal passages are too narrow. Any sign of opening and closing of the nostrils also indicates narrowed nasal passages, and thus constricted breathing. Normally speaking, nostrils should hardly move at all when breathing in and out. It is not a good sign if nostrils move inward on inhalation and outward on exhalation as it points to excessive resistance during breathing. This may improve as the dog grows bigger and its nostrils grow. However, there can never be any guarantee of this, and it is a distinct disadvantage if you plan for your boxer to be a working dog. Sometimes the opening and closing of nostrils is absent in adult dogs at rest, but reappears when they become excited.

Eyelids

Boxers' eyelids are another area of concern. An eyelid should enclose the eyeball, but boxers suffer frequently from

A boxer that greets you like this gets the attention it needs

This pup's nostrils are too narrow

drooping, or rolled-out, lower eyelids, which can be easily identified if the dog looks at you and the red inner lining of the eyelid is visible. The eyelids are meant to protect the eyeball from any incoming foreign matter; a drooping eyelid creates a collection point for dirt and bacteria. Consequently, a drooping lower eyelid is often accompanied by conjunctivitis, in which a green, sometimes even pus-laden, discharge collects in the corners of the eye; this is particularly noticeable in the morning. The eyelids can also roll inward (entropion), causing the eyelashes to rub against the eyeball. This action irritates and reddens the eyeball. In dogs, the eyelid has to be lifted up slightly in order for you to see the whites of the eyes. Inspect the whites of the eyes for any redness before making a purchase and look at how the eyelids close. The inside of an eyelid should show a healthy pink color. Redness indicates irritation.

This non-purebred boxer has a slightly longer nose than normal, and wide nostrils

Feces

A healthy pup will not suffer from gastrointestinal problems. Do not be too embarrassed to take a look at the pup's anus and its feces. Pups that are only just making the transition to solid food often have semi-loose stools. There is nothing wrong with that. However, pups' feces should be solid by the time that solid food forms the principal part of their diet. Runny or even oatmeal-like feces in pups older than seven weeks indicates that their digestive system is not working as well as it should. It is not usually possible to verify the cause, but discuss it with the breeder anyway. In fact, reputable breeders are usually the first to broach the subject. It may be that something needs changing in the pup's diet, but more serious causes may also underlie the problem. For example, worm infestation could be one reason for intestinal problems.

A reputable breeder will raise pups in a clean environment with relatively little excreta on view. If you encourage the pups to play, they will probably need to answer a call of nature immediately afterward. This phase will soon pass.

Which pup suits you best?

Now that you have decided to buy a boxer puppy, the thing is to

Signs of eye irritation are reddened eyes and weeping

This boxer's left eyelid is swollen

*Young pups
should be placed
in a clean
whelping box*

get one that suits you. It must have the sort of character that you want as well. Do you want a fine house dog that gets on well with children, or must your dog also be able to hold his ground in the show ring or as a guard dog? In an ideal world a certified canine behavioral analyst will have performed behavioral tests on the entire litter. This analyst will also have produced a short report on each pup containing recommendations for the owner-to-be. A dog that rates as the average in the litter is usually the best one. Excessive dominance, wariness, or anxiety often lead to objectionable behavior, quite frequently accompanied with aggression toward other dogs or people. Most people will be looking for a boxer that will make a fine house dog. This means that he must not make a dash for the postman if you have left the door open and unattended in a moment of distraction. In such an instance, too strong or domineering a character is not so very desirable. Dogs like this are often troublesome when around other dogs, and harder to train as well. Anxiety is not at all good for a house dog: unforeseen events happen all the time in a family setting and if your dog is completely unnerved on each occasion he will become quite a worry. Behavioral assessments can clarify issues like these.

Behavioral assessment

Official behavioral assessment lies beyond the scope of this book, but there are enough things that you can be alerted to for you to make the right choice. The best age to perform these tests on pups is at seven weeks.

• **Attentiveness**

Crouch down and try to attract the dog's attention to you with friendly calls and tapping on your leg. An unrestricted pup that is not growing up isolated in a kennel will come to you easily. If this is successful, go a stage further and try to keep the pup's attention while slowly walking away. Tractability indicates trust in humans. Anxiety is the very opposite of what you want and you must never take a frightened pup. The possibility always exists that something has gone wrong in the socialization process—a situation that the average dog-lover cannot hope to reverse.

• **Playing and retrieving**

Try playing with the pup a little and, while doing so, throw a toy away some distance (if there are no toys, use a piece of material with a knot tied in it or something else that is comforting for the pup to hold on to). Any reaction to your game should be regarded as excellent, especially if the pup brings the toy back to you.

• **Lying on its back**

Try placing the pup on its back, briefly holding it with one hand over its chest. How does the pup react? Pups with an inclination toward dominance will put up intense resistance and may attempt to bite you. These pups are often rather more difficult to bring up. If you have young children, this type of dog will not have the appropriate character traits. The pup may fare better as a house dog if he soon gives up the fight. If the pup is very anxious (tail between the legs and even urinating) a boisterous family might be just too much for the little fellow.

• **Emotional recovery**

A stable dog remains undaunted by unexpected events. The degree of recovery immediately afterward should tell you something about this. For example, you could try dropping a bunch of keys behind the pup. The pup may be a little startled, but does it recover from the surprise quickly? Ideally, the pup should be only slightly startled, afterward turning round to investigate the keys.

Anxiety is impractical for a house dog

*If he brings the
toy back, it's a job
well done*

Seeking out a working dog

If you want to train your dog for working situations, you will need to look for different character traits. The true working dog is distinguished from a house dog by not capitulating too quickly and not being too cautious. When seeking out a working dog, it is sensible to look especially closely for the following qualities:

• **Good motivation for searching and retrieving**
Spontaneous retrieval is the surest sign that the dog is a willing worker.

• **Perseverance**
You can test this by keeping a toy just out of reach so that the pup has to do its very best to get at it. If the pup tries hard, everything is fine. However, the prognosis is not as good if it gives up after only a few seconds.

• **Insensitivity to pain**
Test this by giving the web of skin between the toes a quick pinch. All is fine if the pup fails to squeal, even if you pinch harder.

*A good family
dog accepts
commands
without fuss*

Other demands are placed on a good working dog

• Indifference to loud noises

You can test this by dropping a can containing a few marbles on the ground. The ability to stay calm under the sound of gunshot is a recurring component in training programs for working dogs.

Pain threshold and young children

If a dog has to grow up with young children, it helps if it is not too sensitive to pain. A higher pain threshold means that it will not feel threatened as quickly if a young child treats it roughly. Proper training can help a great deal with this. If this higher pain threshold is coupled with a compliant character (retrieval and tractability in the tests), you will have the makings of the ideal family dog.

Above all, the boxer is a family dog

5 BEFORE THE PUP ARRIVES AT HOME

The collar

Young pups need a supple leather collar that is not too big. A collar is the means by which you make contact with your pup. A suitable collar communicates your signals clearly. Moreover, you will not be running the risk of your little puppy escaping from its leash in a moment of distraction. There is no point in buying a larger size. You will have to buy several collars in any case before your pup is fully grown.

Why not a choke or check chain?

Nowadays, the preference is not to use check chains in bringing up your dog, however small the chain. A pup can be trained perfectly without resorting to a check chain. Furthermore, check chains appear more likely to cause spinal injuries to the neck over the long term.

The check chain is still used widely by dog trainers, even with young pups. Trainers often enthusiastically liken the way the check chain works to the corrective nip to the neck that the dominant dog in the pack gives to a subordinate. However, this comparison is not really satisfactory. Firstly, we want to prevent long-term physical scarring, and that is not always the

A collar and leash are preferred when training a young dog

Things can get wild when playing

case in nature. Secondly, we are smarter than dogs. In other words, if it can be done in a nicer way, why not do it nicely?

Eating and drinking vessels

It goes without saying that you have to give your pup food and water too. Capacious, tough containers that cannot be destroyed by chewing and gnawing are ideal. Heavy metal bowls fit the bill perfectly. Ceramic bowls are less perfect: boxers will keenly and noisily tip over bowls you have been too slow to refill, and ceramic bowls do not cope well with such treatment. Plastic bowls are gnawed on almost without exception during the puppy stage, with the attendant risk that the pup will swallow some of the plastic. Considering the amount of money that your veterinarian will then require from you, you are better off buying the very best quality bowls you can find.

Advice
Place feeding bowls next to the pup's sleeping quarters. This will help your new puppy acclimatize more quickly to its new home.

The dog crate

A crate is a wire cage or fiberglass box that you can use to keep your pup safe and secure for a period of time. It is an important aid to training your dog. Since it allows you to keep your dog safely enclosed for a while, it prevents the dog from breaking anything when you cannot be there to supervise. It is

Metal bowls are the most appropriate for boxers

also an excellent tool for teaching a pup to be home alone. The training chapter discusses this in more detail. A crate is a relatively expensive purchase, but is more than worth the investment. A pup that has discovered the joy of wrecking your household possessions will cost you far more money in the end.

Sleeping quarters

When your young boxer arrives at your home, he will need his own spot where he can sleep in peace. It is best to put his crate on that spot. Place a blanket in the crate, possibly within a cardboard box so that the pup feels even more protected. It is even better if you can take a piece of material from the pup's litter basket, which will contain a familiar, confidence-boosting scent. Wicker or plastic baskets are not the most appropriate ones to start out with. Pups are quick to chew on anything and everything in their environment. Wicker baskets

The crate is a safe place where the pup can rest

At first, do not leave a pup for hours alone in a crate

are soon ruined. Plastic baskets are more resistant against gnawing, but a young pup can still become very sick after ingesting any plastic. A cardboard box will not last long either, but the advantage is that it can be easily replaced. Moreover, no harm is done if the pup swallows any of it; any cardboard is simply excreted naturally.

Toys

Boxer puppies are incredibly energetic dogs. In order to channel their energy, you will need a great many durable or even indestructible toys. In addition, they love to gnaw on things and thus there must be enough rawhide chews and other chewing toys for them. Toys are not only for your dog's enjoyment, but also become important later as rewards and as a means of holding your dog's attention when training. Toys can help turn a capricious pup into an enthusiastic companion. In theory, anything can serve as a toy, notwithstanding a few initial considerations: naturally, the toy must be safe, and it may not resemble too closely anything that you use yourself—otherwise the pup will be tempted to treat your possessions like toys. For example, old leather shoes are often extremely attractive to a dog. They have an interesting scent and are a good fit in the mouth. Unfortunately, your new shoes will hold the same fascination, and a young pup is cer-

tain to sink his teeth into them a few times. Therefore, do not give your pup any worn-out shoes, old brushes, or other household items to play with.

Suitable toys

Footballs can injure young dogs

Suitable toys
The following toys can be used safely.

Rope (teething) toys: thick cotton ropes with a few knots in them are ideal for tugging games and general romping about. They are also ideal when incorporated as a toy in training sessions. Not all such ropes are of the same quality, however. Some of them have too many loose threads that the dog may swallow, leading to possible gastrointestinal problems. Therefore, buy only the best.

Rawhide toys: there are all kinds of chews, balls, and mini-Frisbees on the market made from rawhide. These types of toy are excellent and quite essential for young pups. Ensure that the rawhide is large enough. Smaller pieces may otherwise be swallowed and cause problems.

Long bones: these chews, made from long bones of cattle, are hard as nails and hardly splinter at all. They are often smoked, making them especially attractive to dogs. They are good for the development of the teeth, particularly when a pup's adult set starts to come through.

Squeaky toys: rubber toys that squeak when squeezed can make dogs deliriously excited, and that is certainly the case with boxers. Hide them discreetly for a while if all the squeaking gets too much. Only buy good-quality toys.

Balls: you should practice a little caution with balls because they can bounce off in all directions. Your pup can easily injure itself in its enthusiasm to get hold of the ball. Placing the ball inside an old, long sock and then knotting it puts an end to any unexpected rebounds.

Long bones and knuckle bones

Only ever give your dog bones bought from a pet store or cattle bones from the butcher that you then roast at home slowly (for several hours). Small bones, especially those from chickens or other poultry, splinter very badly, which can result in serious internal problems, such as gastrointestinal bleeding. Pig bones are sometimes a cause of Aujeszky's disease, which is fatal to dogs. Care should also be taken with slices of marrowbone, as these can become firmly wedged in the lower jaw, especially in the case of young dogs whose jaws are still relatively small.

Sticks and branches are not the most suitable items for play

Variety

Change the toys twice a week for other toys, and hide the ones the pup had been playing with. The same toys will keep their interest if the pup sees them for only a few days each week. An "old" toy will be as good as new again a week later. However, this does not apply to chewing toys. Pups have a huge urge to chew and dog chews should be available to them at all times.

Purpose of toys

Some boxers have a tendency to slobber a great deal if always rewarded with morsels of food during training. A toy makes an ideal alternative to this. Toys can be used for different purposes in training. They not only serve as rewards, but are also a good distraction from something that might compete for your dog's attention, such as another dog or a rabbit on the run. Perfect obedience can be achieved in part by using toys correctly when training. Dogs learn faster when they get something out of the exercise. When training, the toy that your dog loves most is the best one to use as a reward. Let him play with it for a while whenever he has done something really well, but it should not be given at the drop of a hat.

*Boxers have few
problems with
being left alone at
home*

6 REARING
AND BEHAVIOR

More than teaching obedience

Rearing a dog is more than just making him obedient. A pup
must grow up to be a steady, stable dog. Bringing up a boxer
is no picnic. Boxer puppies are extremely endearing and it is
very hard to stand firm even when they have been forbidden
to do something. Add to this their exceptionally adventurous
character, and you will soon realize that you have your hands
full. Consequently, training a boxer requires a firm hand, but
with quite a sense of humor attached. Despite their exube-
rance, the boxer is not such a difficult dog, and punishing
excessively will not make your job any easier.

Being consistent

Being consistent is the most difficult thing of all—that is, until
you experience its benefits. Training goes much faster and
more easily if you direct things with a firm hand. Note that
this is rather different than acting with an iron hand! When
you set your rules conscientiously and keep to them, your dog
will adapt to them quite quickly and not put them constantly
to the test. The further his training progresses, the more easi-

*Boxers have a
humorous side*

ly this is accomplished. However, if he sometimes succeeds in breaking the rules, he will keep trying to break them. The result will be a dog that is a poor listener in difficult situations—and the people around you will not always be delighted by the presence of a boxer that fails to obey commands. This impressive breed can overawe, or even instill fear, if not brought under control.

Being fair

A dog must be able to understand what it is you expect of him, and it must lie within his capacity to carry out properly what you ask him to do. Do not demand that he does certain things well if he has had little practice. Neither should you ever punish a dog for misdemeanors after the event unless you have actually caught him in the act. However, learn from the experience and ensure that he no longer gets the opportunity to flout the rules. All of this can be done without resorting to a great deal of punishment or physical means. Be fair when assessing what a dog is really capable of and what he is not yet ready for. All too often people like to believe that a pup knows "darn well" what is allowed and what is not. In reality this is usually not the case. Young dogs are often given too many opportunities to make mistakes, which is precisely what makes it hard for them to understand what is allowed. Pulling on the leash is one example. Many people teach "walking at heel" exhaustively on the training field, but will permit their dog to pull on daily walks. How then is a young dog to know when he is allowed to pull on the leash and when not? Dogs will keep on doing this until an advanced age if it has been regularly permitted. Punishment by tugging hard on the leash will not change this at all. Consistently teaching the dog to walk with a slack leash will. Training a young dog takes a good year, assuming that you work hard on it too.

Socialization

Perhaps the most important thing of all in the life of a dog is its proper socialization during puppyhood. A dog can be made obedient at any age, but a dog that is poorly socialized will always remain a problem dog.

Socialization means that the pup learns who he is and what his world is like. This cannot be done at any age. Newborn pups are deaf and blind and are aware of what is going on around them only to a limited degree. Their whole focus is on keeping warm, eating, and growing. Young pups' ears and eyes start to function properly between their eighteenth and twentieth days of life. Gradually, from that point onward, they start to observe more of the world about them. The period between opening their eyes and their seventh or eighth week of life is when they learn who their litter companions are. This period is referred to as the primary socialization

Looking away may indicate insecurity

A pup learns early on who the members of his pack are

phase. Its brothers and sisters, along with its mother, form the central image of what the pup sees as its kin. Human contact is also indispensable. If a pup has seen no humans in this period, it will develop an extreme phobia toward them. Therefore, regular contact with the breeder and other people is extremely important. The pup must learn that people are also "its kin."

Bonding

A dog is a pack animal by nature and thus has a bond with its own kind. Pups that have been badly socialized do not have any bond with humans and will shy away. Without bonding, a dog will flee from you and run away. In extreme cases this is referred to as kennel syndrome (see box). Obedience training

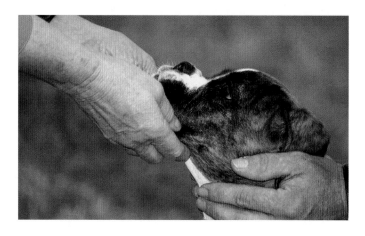

A properly socialized dog can accompany you anywhere

is impossible because the dog needs a natural bond for this to succeed. Why else would a dog be prepared to follow you? Or come to you?

Kennel syndrome
Pups raised at a dog kennel without human contact become extremely anxious. They will do anything to evade people and without an escape route will go rigid with fear. Teaching this category of dog to accept humans as social partners is no longer possible. Consequently, they are totally inappropriate as house dogs. At best, a dog like this can be "tamed" like a wild animal, but it will never become a companion.

Secondary socialization phase

The period from eight weeks onward is referred to as the secondary socialization phase. The world in which a pup lives becomes slightly larger and it begins to discover more about its environment. What should I be wary of? What does me no harm?

It is in this phase that a pup must be brought into contact, calmly and pleasantly, with everything and anything. Everything from busy traffic and crowds of people to boardwalks, smooth tiled floors, and cows and horses. Let your interpretation of "everything" be as broad as possible. The more a pup sees in this period, the more the pup can lump everything together and perceive it as normal. However, protect your dog from negative experiences, because these will remain just as deeply ingrained in its memory. Just let everything take its course gradually.

Never comfort the dog!

An occasion may arise when your pup is startled by something. Never comfort the pup because this will only confirm the fear it feels. For the same reason, never let the pup see that you are startled or scared of something; you are the pup's great role model. Ideally, you should ignore the incident or event, and try to divert the pup's attention toward something fun, such as a toy, a game with a reward, or, in the final instance, by just continuing the walk without too much ceremony. At some other time, try to eradicate the pup's fear by acquainting him once again with whatever it was that scared him, but under controlled circumstances. Do this from a good distance, and gradually get closer. In the case of loud

Make sure that a dog from a kennel is sociable and relaxed in its behavior

noises, try training the pup with muffled bangs at some distance.

Staying home alone starts with the crate

Some breeds have a bad reputation when it comes to being left at home on their own. Fortunately, boxers do not fall into that category. Often this inability to stay at home alone is closely connected to a fear of abandonment; the boxer has a stable character, which makes it relatively simple to teach them to feel secure at home. Doing this begins with proper crate training. The crate must be a safe place for the dog. He can be put at ease by giving him food in or next to the crate from the start and arranging his sleeping quarters there. The best location for a crate is in a quiet corner, from where the pup is able to see the whole room. At the same time, make sure that the dog sees as little as possible of what is happening outside. The pup must be truly able to withdraw into his crate and not be continually tempted to react to his environment. Barking at passing traffic or passing pedestrians will only intensify and it is exceptionally difficult to break the habit. Your neighbors will take a dislike to your dog with good reason if it keeps barking for longer each time. So prevent it.

Crate training

Your pup will still need time to settle in during the first week after his arrival at your home. For the first few nights just let the pup sleep next to your bed in the crate so that he can get used to the crate in a safe environment. During the day, put

the crate in its location in the living room. The pup will always want to sleep whenever he has played, eaten, or returned from a walk. This is the time to enclose him in the crate for a while, while staying in his vicinity. Let him out if he wakes up, and before he has time to make any fuss. Maintain this routine over the next few weeks, so that the pup accepts it as normal. Gradually extend the period that the dog spends in the crate. Carefully note the length of time that he puts up with it. At a later stage, you can use this information to judge how long you can leave him alone. Soon you will be able to leave the house for a while to run some quick errands.

Extend "crate time" only slowly

Do not leave a young dog alone for long too soon. Once boredom ensues, all the success achieved will be quickly undone. Minor discomforts, such as pressure or thirst, make a dog restless and provoke howling and barking. A water bowl in the crate usually gets tipped over, so if you are away only for a short time (up to half an hour) it is better not to put any water in the crate. Be content with things as they are if everything is going well, and extend periods of confinement only gradually. A toy chew can provide some distraction and prevent restlessness. Certainly, older pups need less sleep and are often extremely lively, which is another reason not to increase the time an animal spends in its crate too quickly to over an hour or an hour and a half.

Housetraining

In theory, pups are already housetrained from a very young age insofar as they do not like to foul their own "nest." Pups at four weeks of age are usually already relieving themselves outside their litter basket. The art to housetraining is in preventing mistakes. If a pup has urinated somewhere once, it will be keen to return to the same spot again. Thus the first time matters more than any other. When your pup arrives at your home, first let him urinate wherever it is allowed over the next few weeks—in the yard, for example. Wait patiently until he has done so. Subsequently, let the pup out for a while every hour to repeat the performance so that he has almost no opportunity to make any mistakes. Accidents indoors should never be punished, but cleaned up and ignored instead.

When to urinate?
Pups always have to spend a moment urinating if they have been romping about, playing, or if they have eaten. They will also need to go outside for a while on waking up.

Once used to it, your pup will like withdrawing into his crate for a while

Boxers are extremely devoted dogs

Being let out at night

It is not much fun getting out of bed in the middle of the night to put your pup outdoors. However, if you can bear it, you will be doing good. The more accidents you prevent, the better. Many pups are only able to control their needs throughout a whole night at around twelve weeks of age. They will be able to control themselves sooner if you let them out late at night and once again very early in the morning. Pups aged about seven weeks require you to set the alarm clock at night. As the weeks progress, gradually let the pup out a little later each time. At ten weeks of age, a pup will be able to last out a short night, and at twelve weeks it can manage a regular night. You may have to grit your teeth and bear it for a while, but the rewards are worth it.

"Newspaper housetraining"

For those of you who just cannot manage getting up each night, you can always opt to have your pup do its business on a newspaper, meaning that you need only clean up messy newspapers each morning. However, there is a disadvantage with this method. It may take longer for the pup to start urinating outdoors, because he prefers to do it on "his" newspaper. If you decide to use the newspaper method, then do it only at night. Tidy up newspapers during the day and let your puppy out frequently. When approached in this way, the newspaper method can make for a reasonable interim solution.

Pups like to do their business in a set place

Springing up at people

Boxers do rather a lot of jumping about by nature. This can become a nuisance, as not everyone is prepared for their size and force. Consequently, you must break your dog's habit of springing up onto you or other people as soon as you can. The best way is by physically ignoring it. As soon as the dog makes to spring up against you, turn away from him and look away, emphasizing this with a spoken "No!" or "Bad!" Calmly reward the dog once he has remained on the ground for a few seconds. Persistent springers usually give up if you keep the leash under your foot, which, logically, prevents any upward movement. Sometimes, raising your knee helps as well, but never forget to reward good behavior. If your dog sits spontaneously, then he is a really "good boy." Sometimes it helps if you buckle under, but this can make some boxers so excited that they jump up onto you again and knock you over. See how your dog reacts and decide whether to stand upright or drop to the ground.

*A calm but
attentive attitude
is very promising*

7 OBEDIENCE

All dogs must obey

Today's society has precious little sympathy for disobedience in dogs, and rightly so. In general, dogs may not run free in public spaces, such as city parks and gardens. However, dogs can also cause a lot of trouble when on the leash. Lunging out on the leash, doing its business on the sidewalk, or defensive behavior in crowds of people can all result in painful situations for you or your dog. Basic obedience is as essential as proper socialization, and simply involves calmly accompanying you on the leash, coming to you on your command, and remaining calmly sitting or lying down if that is what you expect. In the end, the idea is for the dog to perform all these actions well under virtually all circumstances. To achieve this, training starts when a pup is still very young and in a variety of situations. Eventually you will need to perform these basic exercises under difficult circumstances so that your dog becomes a reliable partner whatever the situation.

Exercises and commands

Modern training techniques frequently employ the principle that the dog must learn the exercise first and then the command that relates to it. This is in contrast to the past, when the command was issued first, after which the dog had to learn how to carry out the related exercise with a lot of assistance. The new method has a few advantages. First of all, many dogs

*He will love
accompanying
you on all your
outings*

do not understand precisely what the idea is at the beginning. By giving the command first, and coercing the dog to execute it faultlessly afterward, it was inevitable that compulsion sometimes entered the equation. Finally, the dog understood what the idea was only when he responded to the command correctly immediately afterward, possibly with a lot of help. With the modern approach, the desired response is elicited first, followed straightaway by a reward. If the dog can carry out the exercise smoothly, it will not take him long to perform the desired action when a command is given as well. This method quickly familiarizes the dog with the meaning of the command, without it having to endure making many mistakes—and without the involvement of force.

Sitting

Without saying anything, hold a dog biscuit in your closed fist and move this slowly right above the dog's head. The dog will smell the biscuit and follow your hand with his nose. Nine out of ten dogs will then sit of their own accord. Once your dog responds in this way, give him the biscuit and reward him with a friendly sounding "Good boy." After a few times, the dog will start sitting quickly in confident expectation that your fist will open to produce a tasty biscuit. Only now is it the moment to introduce the associated command. As soon as you sense the dog is about to sit down, call out "Sit!" Once he is sitting, open your hand and give him his reward. From that moment onward, reward him only when he sits down imme-

diately after the command "Sit." You may still use a hand motion to assist with this. The advantage of this method is that you teach him to sit without pressure or stress. He will learn faster because he experiences the result of his behavior without coercion, and he will be far more likely to respond in the same way always. He will also enjoy his training exercises with you much more, which reduces teaching time quite considerably. You will produce a more obedient dog as a result.

Attentiveness is the basis for all exercises

When forced, a dog will prefer not to obey, or will have conflicting feelings about obeying at the very least.

Attentiveness

The basis for all obedience is attentiveness. A dog that pays attention to you will learn from you. A dog that pays more attention to his surroundings than to you will learn from you only with difficulty. Together with the socialization process discussed in the previous chapter, attentiveness exercises form the basis for a dog's entire training.

The first stage

Take the pup to a quiet field without distractions. Put an ordinary leash on him and, with the leash in your hand, walk calmly away without saying anything. Reward the pup straightaway as soon as he looks up and walks with you. Do not expect to walk more than a few yards the first few times. He will become especially alert as a result of you walking on a little and then rewarding him. You will soon be able to extend his attention span. It really is a case of building it up second by second, from one second to two, and onward to five and then ten. Never ignore an opportunity to reward the pup for his attention. It will usually take two or three such training sessions before he realizes that he has to keep his eye on you and what you do.

It is important not to say anything to the pup when you walk off. The pup must learn to fix his attention on you spontaneously, and that doing so is rewarding. You must not go to any

Few dogs pay much attention to their owner spontaneously

trouble to get his attention. The rule of thumb as far as attentiveness exercises are concerned is that the more effort you make, the less effort your pup has to make.

The next stage

Once your pup is walking with you attentively for thirty seconds at a stretch, it is time to move on to a busier environment and start from scratch. A few passers-by or a dog at some distance is distraction enough. These minor distractions will make it a little harder for him. Start walking as soon as his attention wanders from you. If your dog follows and looks up at you, out comes his reward again: a "Good boy!" from you and a small treat. Gradually build up to thirty seconds of undivided attention. It is quite possible to achieve this, even with a young pup. Once things are going smoothly, he will be

Everything can be taught with patience and understanding

ready for a little test. Put the pup on a light leash a few yards in length.

The long leash

This longer leash gives the pup more time to do his own thing and thus make the wrong decision by not paying attention to you. Step away again in the hope that the pup will follow you. In all probability he will, because after the previous exercises he will not know any better. Reward him enthusiastically immediately afterward. If his attention is still momentarily distracted, turn around, walk toward him, and then walk past him. He will fix his attention on you because of walking right by him. If he performs well, reward him again straightaway. Progressively increase the time taken just as before.

Attentiveness is not the same as "walking at heel"

These attentiveness exercises must not be confused with walking at heel, which means that the dog is walking in tight formation alongside you, usually on your left. In attentiveness exercises it does not matter which side of you the pup walks. Many young dogs will walk behind you because that way they are in a good position to monitor your movements. It is often an expression of good intentions and intelligence. Another thing about walking at heel is that a dog is expected to come to heel only after you have given a command for him to do so.

All attention fixed on the owner

Walking at heel

Once your pup is paying enough attention to you, you can move up a level. The time has come to start on walking at heel. The preliminary techniques for getting a dog to walk at heel closely resemble the ones used in the attentiveness exercises. This time, however, you do not walk away randomly, but in a specific direction, with your alert pup immediately coming to walk with you on your left, his head roughly level with your body. Commands are not given at first. From now on, you reward the pup only when he walks on your left. Do not make it too difficult for him at first, always walking in a way that makes your left-hand side the most logical position for the pup to take. It should go without saying that you reward the pup enthusiastically and straightaway whenever this happens. Afterward, gradually increase the time for the exercise by a few seconds. The pup will soon keep to your left in anticipation of his reward.

Training in a group

The next stage

The next stage is a little harder. You do not help him to keep walking on your left, but instead you walk for longer stretches straight ahead, encouraging your pup to follow you correctly for longer. Now and then you can also make a turn to the right, so he has to accelerate slightly round the bend to keep up with you. Do not allow him too much leash when doing this to prevent him from crossing behind you and coming out on your right side. Reward him straightaway when he performs a turn correctly. Keep building up the time taken. Once all this is going smoothly, the next phase can commence. Start making turns to the left and right at random, and a little later make a complete 180-degree right turn, so that the pup has to step up his pace sharply to keep level with your legs. These variations make and keep the young dog alert and ensure that he continues to keep his attention on you. Once these exercises are proceeding well, you can start to introduce a few distractions as before.

Boxers are usually friendly when greeting smaller dogs

Once your boxer is consistently walking at heel, introduce the "heel" command, and use it frequently when he is walking at heel, so that he understands its meaning. Then, if you want him to walk by your side, all you need to do is call "heel," and he will do so.

Turning has a purpose

Turning has a purpose and it is not employed arbitrarily. If a dog is constantly walking half a step ahead of you, treat him to a 90-degree turn to the left, thereby heading him off. As a result, he will learn to keep back a step and yield to you. The notorious "front runner" can be dealt with by walking in a circle counterclockwise. By doing this, you remain in the dog's way, and he automatically keeps one step back. The more stubbornly the dog wants to walk ahead of you, the tighter you make the circle. If you become dizzy, just make a quick turn in the opposite direction. This both keeps the dog alert and cures you of your dizziness. Keep expanding the size of the circle if the exercise is progressing well. The ingrained front runner that walks more than one step in front of you can be corrected by making a turn to the right. If he corrects himself without the leash becoming taut, reward him enthusiastically as before. Conversely, a dog that stays at heel correctly will not go wrong with a 180-degree turn to the left. He cannot easily make a mistake, because you are keeping one step ahead of him and are able to give him additional encouragement to follow you.

> **The 80 percent rule**
> If your dog follows your commands 80 percent of the time, you can assume that he understands what you expect of him. If he fails to reach that percentage, his competence level is insufficient and he will often simply not understand you. Punishment often has the opposite effect on dogs of this type and makes them perform worse rather than better. If your dog performs above this level, it is time to start work on some fine-tuning.

Only dogs that listen properly can be given maximum freedom

Always reward a pup when he comes to you spontaneously

Only once a dog responds automatically do you introduce the command "come"

The command "come"

A great deal is involved in getting a dog to learn to come to you swiftly under all circumstances. However, no exercise is as much fun or makes so deep an impression as a dog that comes to you on command, swiftly and without faltering. Moreover, you can award your dog maximum freedom once you are certain that he will come to you straightaway without fail. A dog like this can be released in places where he can work off his energy for a while, without causing a nuisance in those surroundings. You lay the foundations for this exercise when your dog is still a very young pup.

Teaching pups to come

Pups seek safety with their mothers. You take on that role once a pup arrives at your home, and you will benefit from the need for safety by instilling in your pup the principles of coming to the owner in your pup. Pups will regularly seek you out during a walk. Reward this each time with enthusiasm and a tasty snack. You will find that the pup will soon approach you more often and ever more readily. Nevertheless, you should *absolutely not* use the "come" command in this phase. You may move on a stage once things are progressing well. When you see the pup advancing in your direction, hunker down and call out his name invitingly. In addition, show him his favorite toy. You may introduce the "come" command if the pup comes to you quickly and is not distracted on the way by the very first fly to zoom past him. Now is the time to ensure that the pup will definitely come to you when you use the command.

Introducing the "come" command

This phase again requires you to hunker down invitingly with a snack or favorite toy. Call your dog's name and, if he approaches you at top speed, invitingly call out his name and "come!" Keep the command going until the pup reaches you. This enables you to reward the pup straightaway at the end of your command. In other words, this means that you call your pup to you only when he is also close to you. Greater distances make it unnecessarily difficult for the pup, endangering the success of the exercise in the process. Increase the distance slightly over time, but continue to call only when you are quite certain that he will come. Note: at this stage of training, never leash your pup just after calling him to you. He may perceive it as a punishment, which will soon reduce his impetus to come to you swiftly. If you want to put your pup on a leash, do it in some unguarded moment or when you want to end a game.

Distractions

Your pup is now familiar with the command "come" and knows that he must then come to you. However, it has certainly not yet become an automatic response. The mere breath of a distraction can divert him from the right path, because, theoretically, each situation with a distraction is a new

Train a dog on a leash where there are distractions

Gently pull the leash in if he fails to obey

situation for your dog. He does not yet know that he must always respond in the same way to your command. By adding some slight distractions to the situation, he will learn how to respond to the command in the same way even under new circumstances.

The lowest level of distraction is in a neutral environment, where the pup will eventually stop paying attention to you for a moment. Add more distractions once he responds well to his name and the command. It now becomes important for the pup to come to you always. To achieve this, put the pup on a long, lightweight leash. If the pup fails to respond to the command, simply pull in the leash, while praising him enthusiastically. He will soon understand that he must still come to you. Repeat this exercise a few times at each training session, but certainly do not overdo it. Beware of demanding too much of your pup simply because you are in a position to coerce him with the leash. The leash is not a means of coercion but a means of preventing mistakes.

Preventing mistakes

In this phase of his training, never call to your dog unless you are completely sure that he will come. With dogs less than a year old, you should consider in advance whether the chance of success comes out at a good eighty percent. Remember

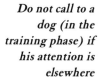

Do not call to a dog (in the training phase) if his attention is elsewhere

always that your calling has no point to it if the dog does not come. By doing so, you only cause confusion. You will just have to go and get him, and treat him calmly and amiably. This will stop your dog from tumbling to the fact that, theoretically, he can get out of following the command. You know he can, but your dog must never know it!

Cutting down on the leash

Most dogs experience the long leash as a means to prevent them from getting out of a situation. You capitalize on this by shortening the leash bit by bit and carrying on as normal with the exercise. Once coming to you has become a conditioned response, i.e. automatic, the leash can come off, and you will have accomplished a great feat of training. Coming to you quickly and readily remains the most difficult training exercise that there is.

Commonly made mistakes (in order of importance)
1: Punishment if the dog comes to you late
2: Failure to reward the dog
3: Introducing too many distractions too soon
4: Leashing the dog as soon as he comes to you

When things go wrong

Dogs will be disobedient at some point or other. Ignore this when it happens and leash the dog. If it occurs again, go back a stage in the training program and repeat a stage that your dog knows by heart. Your dog is less likely to realize that he can avoid following commands if you ignore a mistake. Punishment will only make him apprehensive, causing him to hesitate on the next occasion that he hears the command "come." In the final analysis, you need to get things in perspective. A boxer is a clown capable of great performances. If his clownish nature gets the upper hand for a moment, you can often steer him back on course by playing a game with him. You can bring him back under control a little later.

Lying down

Teaching your dog to lie down is useful if you want the dog to be quiet for a period of time—an exercise that is hardly surplus to requirements in the case of boxers. Begin as follows: hunker down on one knee with the dog alongside you on the outside, as shown in the photograph. Tempt the dog through the "gateway" made by your leg with a dog biscuit held on the inner side. He will have to lie down to get his biscuit. Reward him quickly as soon as he lies down. If he responds to lying down readily, introduce the command "down" or "lie down."

He will definitely lie down for a biscuit

As for their sound, "lie" and "sit" are quite indistinct and when pronounced, the words resemble each other rather closely and might therefore be easily confused by your dog. For this reason, we recommend using a simple command "Down!". The collocation of "Lie Down!" is seen as acceptable, however, you should try to pronounce the words of the command in a distinct way.

Lying down from a standing position

When the dog responds readily to the command, try it again standing upright, emphasizing it with an arm gesture. At first, you will have to stand slightly bent over to make the dog actually lie down; however you will soon be able to maintain an upright posture. To prevent the dog from springing up, it is useful to keep the leash under your foot. This ensures that the dog can only lie down and not make any mistakes. Remember not to give any corrections. Your dog is still in the

preliminary learning phase. Once your dog is lying down, start to increase the amount of time that he has to stay there; this soon transforms lying down into a staying exercise.

Staying

Staying can be divided into two exercises. The first of these is to keep your dog lying down or sitting calmly on one spot. The second exercise consists of having your dog stop whatever it is doing and stand still immediately after you give the command "stay," and then calmly await the next command. All training programs include the first staying exercise. However, the second type is required much more frequently in daily life. In theory, you teach both exercises in roughly the same way.

Begin by getting your dog to lie down or sit quietly, as you wish, while you stand in front of him. For example, build up the exercise first from a lying down position and subsequently from a sitting position, repeating the whole exercise in so doing. At first, you say nothing, but just keep postponing the reward a little more each time so that the dog has to wait a few seconds for it, either sitting or lying down. Gradually increase the time up to approximately thirty seconds. Now say his

Once he grasps the principle, lying down on command is soon learnt

The dog must trust you with an exercise like this

name followed by the command "sit, ... good boy" (spoken softly), and one beat later: "Stay." Then wait patiently for a few seconds and reward the dog again if he stays where he is. Once again, build this up to thirty seconds.

The next stage is not only to get your dog to wait, but for you to take a step backwards at the same time. Praise your dog straightaway after he has stayed still for a few seconds. Subsequently, increase the distance and, afterward, the time taken. You will notice how quickly your dog advances in this phase. It becomes all the more tempting to keep moving furt- her and further away. However, it is preferable first to build up the time to, say, three minutes before you start standing very far off. When he is coping well with this, it is time to introduce distractions again.

Staying put immediately on command

With today's busy traffic, it is extremely useful if your dog stays put as soon as you give the command "stay." Once the above exercises are well instilled, give the "stay" command at unexpected moments, but always ensuring that you have the dog within reach. For example, if your dog wants to overtake you, call out "stay" suddenly, and hold your hand in front of

his nose. Most dogs then respond immediately by sitting or lying down, but if he continues to stand then that is acceptable too. Reward him again straightaway. Some handbooks advise using the command "wait" for the last exercise since the dog is actually being expected to perform a slightly different maneuver.

For its own safety, teach your dog to respond immediately to your commands

A boxer's self-
assured character
makes it an
excellent working
dog

8 BOXERS AS WORKING DOGS

Advanced training

The active, strong character of the boxer makes him extremely appropriate for all types of canine sports. A boxer can actually do anything as long as he is physically healthy and well trained. Consequently, quite a lot of boxer enthusiasts are actively engaged in physical work with their dogs. Because of its stable, work-hungry character, the breed is particularly valued as a working dog in Germany, its country of origin, where the breed is seen particularly widely in Schutzhund training programs, which is to say training programs for guard dogs. The German Schutzhund program is equivalent to the international IPO I, II, and III certificates. IPO stands for

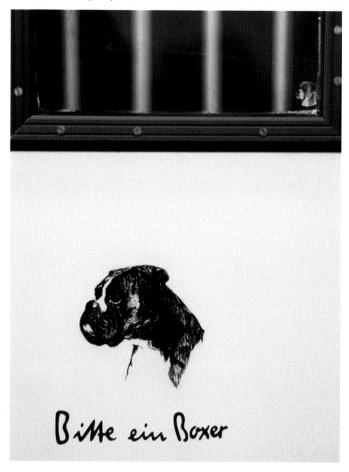

Bitte ein Boxer

Internationale Prüfungs Ordnung and consists of three levels. The IPO program is extremely varied and if that appeals to you, you can enjoy years of training pleasure with your dog.

Is a boxer really suitable for the IPO?

People usually think first about German shepherds in terms of guarding and defensive work for dogs. Devotees of the IPO program choose German shepherds more often than boxers. The reasoning behind this is usually that people can achieve much more with German shepherds. Nevertheless, the boxer combines a number of qualities that make him an ideal guard dog. In the main, they are less aggressive, thus tend not to be so quick to bite as German shepherds. Their stimulus threshold is slightly higher, making them more pleasant to have around as housedogs, despite their training.

Another point of criticism cast at boxers is that their ability as tracking dogs is less because of their short noses. However, this, too, is only a minor handicap. The IPO III examination requires a dog to be able to follow a track left behind an hour before. Virtually all dogs are capable of doing this, subject to gradual growth of skill through training. Ultimately, this is more a question of training than one of physical capacity. For the Tracker Dog Examination, a dog must follow a track left behind three hours before. This is difficult for other breeds as well as boxers. Finally, it should be said that, as a rule, the

Obedience exercises must be trained to perfection

boxer is a faster and more flexible dog than, for example, the German shepherd, which is an advantage in this branch of sport. All reasons, therefore, for mustering a little patience and perseverance if you want to set your boxer to work on this.

The Tracker Dog Examination

Anyone who enjoys active involvement with their dog wants to carry on testing the boundaries, which makes the tracker dog examination an additional challenge. It involves a dog having to complete a track of 1,400 paces, thus about a kilometer long, that is three hours old and on which three objects have been placed. It demands quite a performance from the dog, and circumstances need to be a little in its favor. If your examination day is very windy, it can be really hard going. However, if it is humid, cool, and dead calm, your dog may exceed all your expectations.

Other sports

A boxer is a real doer and giving him an active life makes him a much happier animal. The many different sports that you can

An important quality in a working dog is to enjoy retrieving

become involved in with your dog might have been tailor-made for him. He can perform superlatively in the B & O program (Behavior and Obedience program). Now and then, he will have the odd urge to go on the razzle, but with a keen sense of his character you will be able to compete with your boxer against any other breed. Flyball is something that he can really get to grips with. Boxers are crazy about balls, and capturing the ball rewards their strong retrieving instincts. Hurdles are child's play for them. In fact, Agility is also a highly appropriate sport for this breed. Nevertheless, this sport is becoming increasingly dominated by Border Collies, making the competition less attractive to other breeds. This has resulted in members of boxer clubs initiating their own competitions. This provides a fairer competition, and one that is much more enjoyable for boxer enthusiasts. Finally, boxers are excellent at undergoing the Endurance [Stamina] Test. This tests physical condition with the dog trotting alongside the bicycle over a distance of twenty kilometers (12 miles). This includes three short intervals. At the end, the dog has to complete a simple obedience test.

Are all boxers suitable for sports?

The IPO program is quite intense and not one that every dog will be able to complete successfully. Retrieval work ['pakwerk': literally > grabbing/getting/catching work] requires a dog's courage and self-confidence. It is sometimes recommended in

This could be in store if everything goes well

order to give more self-confidence to dogs that are rather dejected, but, as a rule, retrieval work tends to increases the desire to bite. Dogs with less self-confidence may then revert to this type of taught aggression. In other words, it is best to withhold from this activity with anxious dogs until their self-confidence has increased and obedience has been perfectly instilled. Lastly, the fact is that not all dogs can be motivated to follow very old tracks. It requires a lot of concentration, and boxers do enjoy the distractions of their surroundings now and again.

Physical checks by your veterinarian

Sports make all kinds of demands on a dog. Boxers suffer sometimes from problems with their locomotor apparatus. For that reason, aim for a slow build-up, and have your dog checked by your veterinarian every so often for any physical faults. Medical checks can prevent a mountain of unpleasantness in the long term.

BOXERS AS WORKING DOGS 81

*In addition to
proper food, fresh
water is essential*

9 DIET

Many types

Anyone who is a regular visitor to kennel club events and specialist pet stores will already be familiar with the many types of dog foods that exist. A novice dog owner is unable to see the wood for the trees. The picture is not made any clearer by the many theories in circulation on the subject.

However, it is not as complex as it seems. The pet foods industry is a huge business sector that is involved in a great deal of research. These companies have reputations to keep. They base their foods on the information obtained from research, which means that manufactured pet foods are generally excellent foodstuffs to which, even in the most time-consuming of cases, you only have to add water. Really not so bad after all.

Complete diets

The health of your dog depends on few things more than a good diet. The body needs all kinds of nutrients to help with metabolic processes, such as growth, recovery, and movement. These nutrients consist of proteins, fats, and carbohydrates. These substances are used to build the body, as well as to meet its energy requirements. The digestive system is not able to deal with all foodstuffs equally well.

*Manufactured
foods are wolfed
down*

Biscuit rewards must be counted as part of the day's rations

Some types of food require the body to expend more energy and effort in extracting their nutritional components than others. Dogs are physically unable to extract nutrients from some types of food. Consequently, dogs are unable to break down cellulose from any food with vegetarian content. To make plant-based food digestible for dogs, manufacturers have to process it first. A complete quality food is composed of nutritional components that can be easily and fully absorbed by a dog's digestive system. While a food may well contain a certain dietary component, it is of very little use unless the dog can digest it, and its nutritional value will be lower as a result.

Nutritional value

Scientific literature likes to use the expression "nutritional value." This is the amount of protein (plus vitamins) that a dog can extract from food and convert into body protein.

Different dogs have different energy requirements

This nutritional value varies according to the raw material being used in the food as a source of protein. The lower the nutritional value, the more protein the dog needs to ingest. Protein may not account for more than 30 percent of food content, because this can have long-term physical effects, including kidney damage. For a house dog, a protein level of 24 percent constitutes a high nutritional value. Quality dog foods guarantee a high nutritional value, providing enough protein to meet an animal's physical requirements, while putting less of a strain on the kidneys. This is particularly important for older dogs. A similar situation exists in relation to fats. Food must contain sufficient essential fatty acids to meet the body's needs.

Different brands

The composition of these important nutrients varies according to the brand, but you can be sure that the top brands fulfill all the nutritional requirements and that your dog will not be missing out on anything. Price differences between the diverse brands relate in part to the processing that the food has undergone. This processing makes the food more digestible for dogs, meaning that they need to eat less in order to meet their dietary requirements. Moreover, this also makes a difference to the amount of waste a dog excretes. A second difference is determined by the quality of a food's raw materials. When deciding on a source of protein, a manufacturer may choose remnants, such as offal or fishmeal, but may equally choose to use real meat, such as chicken or lamb. Obviously, the quality of the

All sorts of food and brands: the choice is up to you

food is better when manufacturers use good-quality meat in their products. These more expensive quality raw materials obviously affect the price. In addition, the better manufacturers (which are often global concerns) invest in research and development regarding special dietary needs, such as food allergies, milk substitutes for very young pups, or other foods that benefit animal health. Inevitably, advertising also accounts for a share of the cost.

The better brands have developed foods that take a dog's age into account

Artificial preservatives

Boxers seem to be quite sensitive to artificial preservatives and other additives. For that reason, choose foods that contain natural preservatives. A poor coat, constant scratching and biting of the coat, and other symptoms that indicate skin irritation, can be signs of an allergic reaction.

Types of food

There are dozens of types of food on the market, ranging from fresh deep-frozen products through to canned food and the ever-popular complete dry foods. As a rule, the shelf life of dry foods is the best and these are usually slightly cheaper as well. Fresh food and canned food are usually quite expensive and you should bear in mind that they are largely composed of water anyway. Dogs usually find these foods tastier, but you will be paying a disproportionately high price for the water content. Biscuits keep well, partly because of their very low water content, which makes it practical, and thus more economical, to buy them in bulk. Most dogs will wolf down dry food when you add water or stock to it.

Creatures of habit

The dog is a creature of habit that is not bothered by eating the same biscuits day after day. Once a dog has become used to it, he will usually choose the food he is familiar with above another, if given the choice. He will still show a keen

Dog foods are often a subject of discussion at shows

A steady pace of growth is what a young dog needs

interest in other things, of course, but you can put those other foods to good use as reward items. Changes to the diet can sometimes result in gastrointestinal problems. Therefore, you need not feel at all guilty about giving your dog the same food every day.

Feeding puppies

Special puppy foods are available that are specifically formulated for their growth requirements. These puppy foods are a godsend in the first few months. After six months, however, the greater part of the growth spurt is over, after which you can move a pup on to food for adult dogs. A ste-

Special foods are available for pups

ady pace of growth is important in ensuring that a pup grows properly. Too much food, or food that is too rich, produces too rapid an increase in body weight, putting the skeleton under too much strain. You can prevent a pup from growing too fast and experiencing related complaints, such as growth pains, by moving it on to adult food at the right time.

How much and how often?

Young pups require four meals a day. After four months, reduce this to three meals a day. By six months, this becomes two meals a day, which is what is also recommended for adult dogs. As a result, you can limit the amount of food per meal. You will find information on the quantity of food to give on the food's packaging, which you can use as a rule of thumb. However, in practice, you should feed "by sight": you must be able to feel the dog's ribs distinctly and they

Biting on a branch

should be just visible, otherwise he is classed as overweight. If the pup does not eat up his food straightaway and with gusto, this can also be a sign that you are giving too much. If either of these situations occurs, reduce his portions slightly for the time being and remove the bowl immediately after meals.

When a pup arrives at your home

Pups are very sensitive to changes in diet. Ask the breeder about the food he is giving so that you can use the same one when you take the pup home with you. The transition from the litter to your home can induce stress, which may show up in gastrointestinal problems, such as diarrhea and, sometimes, even vomiting. You may worsen the situation if you change the food during this acclimatization phase.

If you want to change your dog's food, allow a good week to do it in. Your dog will gradually get used to the new food if you mix some of it in gradually with his regular food. Substitute a little more new food each day, mixed in with the "old" food. You can make the full transition to the new food after a week to ten days. Your pup will not miss out on anything if you mix a complete dry food of one brand with that of another during this short period.

An adult dog's nutritional requirements are not the same as those for a pup

Move on to senior dog food at the right time

Older dogs

It is best not to give older dogs food with a high protein content. Proteins are not only used in the body, but are also broken down, which releases urea. The kidneys are responsible for eliminating this harmful substance. High levels of protein lead to higher production levels of urea and thus to a heavier burden on the kidneys. Older dogs' kidneys are quite vulnerable. Dogs that have led a quiet life with just a couple of walks a day should be moved on to "senior" biscuits from the age of seven. These biscuits contain a lower percentage of protein and, naturally, have a high nutritional value. Active dogs consume more protein and can make this transition slightly later in life. However, it is better to put even active boxers on a diet specially developed for older dogs from the age of nine.

> **What a dog is expressly forbidden from eating:**
> - Bones from poultry and game (these can splinter and damage the intestines);
> - Pork products and raw pork can be infected with the Aujeszky virus. This virus leads to Aujeszky's disease, which is usually fatal in dogs;
> - Chocolate products (can make some dogs very sick);
> - Candy/sugar (bad for dogs' teeth)

Dietary problems

In summary, feeding your dog sensibly is not hard to do given the very many excellent foods on the market. This becomes more difficult if the dog is intolerant to a particular type of food, which can often be recognized by a coat that is dull and in poor condition, or by some other disorder (poor appetite, itching, listlessness, or, conversely, extremely manic behavior). If this is the case, have your veterinarian check your dog over before doing anything. These symptoms need not be directly connected with food, but could point to another underlying health problem.

Some dogs bury their bones

Dog chews

Pups' adult teeth start to come through at approximately the age of four months, when they will want to chew on anything and everything. Provide lots of rawhide dog chews. It helps them through teething and prevents damage to your home furnishings.

*Dogs are more
likely to get
parasites in hot
summers*

10 CARE

Coat care

Your work is soon over with a boxer as far as combing and brushing are concerned. You need nothing more than a brush with only moderately stiff bristles, or a rubber brush. Normally, boxers molt twice a year, when you will need to brush more frequently. However, once a week is enough through the rest of the year. Boxers will sometimes shed some hair continuously. This can be dictated by environmental temperature and also by seasonal change with the lengthening or shortening of the day. Nothing much can be done about this molting. It may help if you have your dog sleep in a slightly cooler room, as long as you ensure that the temperature never falls below 59 degrees Fahrenheit (15 degrees Celsius).

No outdoor kennels
Boxers must sleep indoors because, with their shorthaired coats, they are not so good at withstanding the cold.

Teeth

Teeth must be looked after to prevent the build-up of tartar and to counter the explosive growth of oral bacteria. Bad breath in dogs is usually the result of bacteria growing on tartar and at the edge of the gums. Tartar leads to inflammation of

*A rubber brush is
enough to keep a
coat in good
condition*

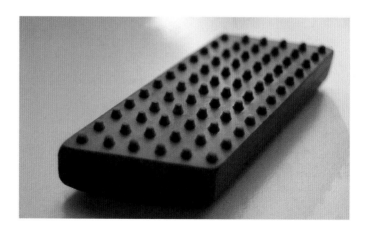

Check teeth regularly

the gums, which in turn can result in the gums receding and an accelerated deterioration of the teeth.

As with most things, pups must learn to get used to dental care from a young age. Dental care involves a number of things and includes cleaning the canines and molars by brushing, removing tartar before it has time to accumulate, preventing it by giving the dog something tough to chew on regularly, as well as food that requires the dog to use its teeth.

Teeth cleaning

Getting a dog used to cleaning its teeth is simple. Young pups do not need much dental care (they have no molars, but they do have premolars), which is precisely why this is the easiest time to get a pup used to all that "rummaging around" in his mouth as pleasantly as possible. Smear some pleasant-tasting food on your finger and gently put your finger in his mouth. He will do his very best to lick your finger clean as you do so. The next stage is to repeat this without the food and to reward him immediately afterward. Next, use a soft children's toothbrush: smear on something tasty and gently put it

Tartar can be removed with a tartar-scraping tool

Physical exercise is important for boxers

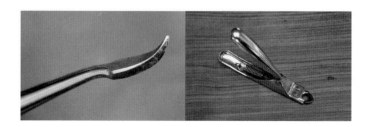

*A special pair of
nail clippers works
very well*

into the dog's mouth. As yet there is still no actual brushing.
Later, gradually start to make gentle brushing movements
until, in the end, you are able to give the teeth a real clean.
Adopting this approach makes teeth cleaning an enjoyable
experience for your dog rather than an annoying one. Dog
toothpastes are available on the market, but children's toothpastes will do just as well. Dogs will not develop cavities if
they are not given sugary foods. This is because dogs lack an
enzyme in their saliva that converts starch into the sugars that
attack the teeth. The primary intention of teeth cleaning is to
prevent the build-up of tartar on the teeth.

Nails

Nail clipping is rarely necessary if a dog is walked regularly
outdoors on hard surfaces. However, there is one exception:
the "dew claw" on the inside of the foreleg. This nail, or claw,
does not touch the ground and thus keeps on growing. Sooner
or later, this long nail will catch on something or other and
tear off. Apart from this being extremely painful for the animal, the wound it leaves behind can become infected, which
is why this nail must be clipped regularly. Boxers with white
forelegs have white nails that allow the part carrying blood
vessels to be clearly seen. This is not the case in boxers with
black nails. The part carrying blood vessels usually extends
¼ inch (6 to 7 mm) along the length of the nail. You must keep
a minimum distance of just under ¼ inch (5 mm) away from
this zone when clipping these nails. In practice, nails are clipped at a distance of ½ inch (11 to 12 mm) measured from the
skin to the cuticle. Special nail clippers from a specialist pet

store are more appropriate for clipping dog nails than ordinary scissors. You are less likely to make a slip when using them.

The eyes

Boxers can sometimes experience problems with their eyes. Many boxers' eyelids bulge out too far, quickly collecting dirt and grime, which can cause eye irritation. This manifests itself in weeping from the corners of the eye and reddened, sometimes inflamed, eyelids, sometimes even including the conjunctival tissue at the inner corner of the eye. The breed standard prescribes that a dog should be "dry" without wrinkling ("dry" is a breeders' term for taut skin). Nevertheless, great value is placed on the appearance of a few wrinkles on the forehead. However, if this is excessive it can mean that the skin covering the head is too loose, resulting in the aforementioned eye problems. (See also: Illnesses and health.)

The ears

Boxers have few ear problems. The ear constantly produces a waxy substance, known as cerumen. Its purpose is to trap any dirt that enters the ear canal thus preventing it from penetrating any deeper into the more delicate parts of the ear. In long- and coarse-haired breeds of dog, hair in and around the external ear forms the first barrier against intrusive grime. However, the hair in short- and smooth-haired dogs like the boxer is of little help against grime and, consequently, the cerumen becomes dirt-laden more quickly. For that reason, it is sensible to check your boxer's ears regularly. If there is an excess of dirty earwax, you can remove it by wrapping a wad of absorbent cotton around your pinkie and carefully cleaning the ear. You should not try to go as deep as possible, nor should you use Q-Tips to clean out the ear canal. Theoretically, the ear canal does not need to be cleaned because the earwax it produces flows outward from it. If the amount of earwax is excessive, put a few drops of salad oil into the ear to dilute the wax slightly and make it easier to remove.

The tail

Many countries no longer permit the docking of boxers' tails, which was once common practice. Since selective breeding never took the appearance of the tail into account in the past, all sorts of different types of tail are now appearing, often, sadly, lacking in strength. Shorthaired dogs with full tails

quite often lash them violently against walls or furniture. Since it is not possible to curb a boxer's tail-wagging, this results in persistent injuries, particularly to the tip of the tail. In some cases, it is sometimes necessary to amputate the tip to prevent further harm. If possible, try to adjust the layout of your home so that your dog has enough space. It is sensible not to greet your dog in narrow doorways but, instead, to move to a spot where he has plenty of space to wag his tail with abandon. This becomes habitual behavior in a dog if done from an early age, with your dog automatically walking to that spot each time to greet you. Bandage the tail straightaway after even the slightest injury to prevent it becoming any worse. At present, there are still quite a number of dogs with these slight, delicate tails. In the long term, breeders will have to do everything they can to breed dogs with robust, shorter tails.

Weeping may indicate eye irritation

Inspect the ears regularly

Removing ticks

The easiest way to remove a tick is with a tick removal tool that can be obtained from specialist pet stores. These are small devices that clasp the tick close to the skin surface. The tick will release its grip of its own accord if you follow the instructions that come with the tool and proceed care-

*Docking is no
longer permitted
in many Western
countries*

fully. Afterward, it may be a good idea to retain and refrigerate the tick for
a month in case any infection develops in your dog and your veterinarian
needs to examine the culprit. Otherwise, destroy the tick to prevent it from
being picked up again later.

Flea prevention

Fleas like to hide in the dense, warmer parts of an animal's
coat. A boxer's short, smooth hair offers little cover to these
pests. They prefer to gather in the groin area, behind the ears,
or in the "armpits." A thorough examination of these areas
will show whether your dog has fleas or not. In particular,
look out for the telltale black granular particles excreted by

these parasites.

A second advantage of short hair is that it makes it more difficult for the fleas to find refuge from pesticides. So, in theory, fleas need not pose a big problem for boxers. However, it is your surroundings that need your particular attention in the event of flea infestation. Flea eggs and larvae frequently end up in any dusty corners, cracks, and ledges in the vicinity of the dog's basket. Regular vacuum cleaning is essential, as is treating these problem areas with appropriate pesticides when you have a flea infestation.

Worms

Fleas can be infected in the larval stage with the "cucumber tapeworm" *(Dipylidium caninum)*. A dog becomes infected on eating any infected fleas, which is why you are recommended to deworm your dog after any flea infestation. In addition to the cucumber worm, dogs can also become infested with roundworm *(Toxocara canis)*. Worse still are increasing cases of trichina worm infestations, and of alveolar hydatid disease (respectively, *Trichinella spiralis* and *Echinococcus multilocularis*). These also pose a serious threat to humans. They are spread by small rodents, such as mice, and the animals that hunt them. For that reason, never let your dog eat any small rodents.

Risk to humans

Children whose faces get licked or who play on a lawn are particularly at risk from contracting a worm infestation. Contact with these parasites can result in allergic reactions or asthmatic complaints. Therefore, deworm your dog every three to four months as a preventive measure.

Vaccination schedule

6 weeks	1st set – Distemper and Parvovirus
9 weeks	2nd set – Repeat against Parvovirus plus Leptospirosis
12 weeks	3rd set – Repeats against Parvovirus and Leptospirosis, plus Infectious Canine Hepatitis, Kennel Cough, and, if necessary, Rabies
16 weeks	Parvovirus or Leptospirosis, if present in your neighborhood
12 months	Repeats against Distemper, Parvovirus, Leptospirosis, Infectious Canine Hepatitis, and Kennel Cough
Annually	Parvovirus, Leptospirosis, Kennel Cough, possibly Rabies, possibly Distemper, according to your veterinarian's advice

11 ILLNESSES AND HEALTH

Life expectancy
Being fed well and properly cared for are the foundations for good health. Nevertheless, all dogs will get sick at some point. Older dogs, in particular, will start to show signs of deterioration. Boxers remain playful and active until late in life (8 to 9 years), but, unfortunately, they can sometimes deteriorate quite rapidly. Consequently, boxers do not live to very great ages—usually no older than 11 or 12 years.

Spondylosis
Old age hits boxers quite hard. This can be seen in the breed's propensity to suffer from degenerative diseases of the joints (arthrosis), particularly along the spinal column (spondylarthrosis or spondylosis). Spondylosis in this area can lead to

An older boxer with cataracts, but still high-spirited

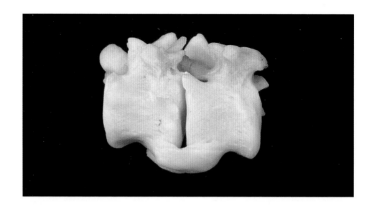

Spondylosis can result in growths on the vertebrae

hook-like projections of bone that put pressure on spinal nerves. This is accompanied by a stiff back, occasionally with considerable pain, very occasionally even with partial paralysis. Even so, a dog will start to be affected only once its condition is causing him serious trouble. Spondylosis is a difficult condition to prevent. However, keep a close watch for early signs of it, such as:
- stiffness when standing up
- stiffness in the morning
- pain without an obvious limp when walking
- difficulty in putting on a sprint

If you observe any of these symptoms, it is time to adjust your dog's physical exercise program, excluding jumping, sprinting, or wild romping about. Long walks are usually still possible and they help to keep the dog in condition. The symptoms of these diseases closely resemble those for hip dysplasia and your veterinarian will have to take an x-ray to make a final diagnosis.

Foreskin infection

Male dogs suffer quite often from chronic foreskin infection. The infection produces a purulent discharge that hangs from the foreskin of the penis in the form of a green droplet. These droplets can leave behind unpleasant stains around your home. Treatment for this condition may involve using an antibiotic ointment. Furthermore, the foreskin must be kept properly clean using, for example, a diluted solution of either hydrogen peroxide or iodine. Naturally, this is far from a pleasant task and often leads to drastic action having to be taken: the problem can be remedied if you have the dog castrated.

Boxers are somewhat prone to cruciate (knee) ligament problems

Cruciate (knee) ligament injuries

Boxers are vulnerable to the tearing of ligaments found within the knee (stifle)—the cruciate ligaments. This injury usually occurs after the age of 2 years and the reasons for it are not always apparent. Accidents or mishaps through physical exertion often play no part in it, with the ligament appearing to have torn almost spontaneously. While the underlying cause is unclear, there are indications that the body initiates a defensive response against its own cruciate ligaments, causing them to weaken and rupture. A genetic predisposition to this is probably involved.

Tumors

Boxers appear to be prone to the development of tumors. This is a significant cause of death among older boxers. Do not allow your dog to put on too much weight, as this will prevent you from recognizing the appearance of unusual lumps and

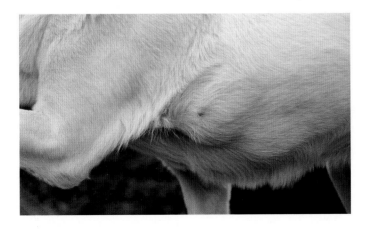

Boxers are prone to tumors: look out for unusual lumps

bumps in good time. Apart from that, it is also better for your dog's skeleton. Fast-growing lumps, lumps that bleed spontaneously, and other strange growths require prompt examination by your veterinarian. Dog tumors can be treated only when caught at an early stage. All older dogs develop warty bumps that often start around the head, but which can appear all over the body. These are not necessarily malignant tumors. Tumors will often grow unnoticed inside the body. For that reason, you should also keep watch for any noticeable changes to your dog's eating habits and bowel movements. Eating either too much or too little is abnormal, especially if your dog is losing weight as well. If a dog's food has not changed, its stools should not suddenly change either. Changes in their color and consistency must be closely monitored, as should the frequency of your dog's bowel movements.

Heart conditions

Inherited disorders often appear only later in life

On average, boxers suffer more from heart conditions than many other breeds. In particular, boxers show above-average incidences of dilative cardiomyopathy (DCM), a heart muscle disorder. The symptoms are an irregular heartbeat, coughing and shortness of breath, weight loss, and, occasionally, beco-

ming acutely sick. Cardiac abnormalities can be life-threatening and therefore these symptoms must be investigated immediately by a veterinarian. Therapy usually consists of drugs with possible dietary adjustments.

Hip dysplasia

Hip dysplasia (HD) is primarily a hereditary disorder in which the ball and socket in the hips do not connect properly. In serious cases, this abnormality can be observed even in young pups, but it usually becomes apparent only in early adulthood. A specialist veterinarian will have to perform a physical examination and take x-rays in order to give you a definitive answer. HD often results in symptoms suggesting arthritis when an animal is only young. As well as being inherited, diet and exercise affect the progress of the condition. Internationally, most breeders' associations insist on x-ray examinations for hip dysplasia. While HD does occur in boxers, it is not a huge problem. There are varying degrees of HD and the more serious types of HD with an early onset appear rarely in boxers. Although boxers are prone to arthritis, this usually appears later in life (after the age of 6 years) and it does not affect the hips alone.

Elbow dysplasia

Elbow dysplasia (ED) is becoming a big problem for a number of breeds. Given the hereditary character of this condition, it is important to screen breeding animals for its presence. Although the condition does appear in boxers, it is not a major health issue within the breed.

Elbow dysplasia is a collective term for a number of different developmental disorders connected with the elbow. Essentially, it relates to various pieces of cartilage that can cause problems within the joint, often because they fail to ossify gradually with the rest of the ulna at approximately $4^{1}/_{2}$ to 5 months of age. This may sometimes occur through a minor trauma, but it can arise spontaneously as well.

An older dog may behave more sedately

As a rule, ED is manifested by the pup showing a significant limp when walking; the elbow is often swollen, sometimes warm to the touch as well, and the pup is in pain.

A veterinarian will include x-rays to confirm the diagnosis. There are different variants of ED, which include:

1. coronoid dysplasia, situated to the anterior of the elbow;
2. anconeal dysplasia, situated to the posterior of the elbow;
3. osteochondrosis dissecans (OCD), in which a loose piece of cartilage occurs in the joint that may cause the joint further damage. Moreover, this variant can also appear in other joints, such as the shoulder;
4. elbow incongruence, in which the ulna and the radius do not grow at the same rate, creating an abnormal alignment and, consequently, producing an abnormal load on the forequarters.

Naturally, any treatment depends on discussions with your veterinarian, but acting quickly with surgery is often desirable and can make the long-term prospects much better. However, your dog's further prognosis also depends on other matters, such as the damage that the elbow joint has already undergone.

Markings on the head around the eyes and ears do not usually indicate disorders

Be prepared for deafness or blindness if a dog's head is (almost) entirely white

If your pup is limping, take it to the veterinarian without a moment's hesitation.

White boxers

Quite a large number of boxers are born white. In some blood lines the percentages for this run up to 20 to 30 percent. The condition is often accompanied by a number of serious problems, of which deafness is the most common. The same applies to dogs with unpigmented ears (i.e. white) —they also often turn out to be deaf. It is possible to examine dogs for this using the specially developed BAER test, which investigates whether the animal is deaf bilaterally (on both sides) or laterally (on one side). White boxers with colored markings around the eyes and on the ears rarely suffer from this disorder. The fact that the rest of their body is white is unimportant. A lack of pigmentation does make dogs very sensitive to sunlight, or, to be precise, the ultraviolet rays from the sun. This is also an irritation for the dog and too much sunlight can lead long term to a greater chance of contracting (skin) tumors. According to the breed standard, no more than one-third of a boxer may be white, which is why you will not come across any white or largely white boxers at shows. If you want to keep a white boxer, perhaps because you had no show plans anyway, discuss at length with the breeder what is to happen regarding the pup and additional expenses in the event that any disorders are discovered. The BAER test can be done while the pup is still with the breeder.

Epilepsy

Boxers are prone to epilepsy, which is often revealed in the breed late in life. Epilepsy is a disturbance in the brain in which the dog has fits and also simultaneously becomes unconscious. It is very unpleasant and upsetting when your dog suddenly goes into a seizure of this sort. This, too, is a condition that requires more thorough investigation, particularly with regard to future breeding policy.

While epilepsy can be suppressed medicinally, this does not mean it is any less of a heavy burden for either the dog or the owner.

Short noses

Bulldogs' truncated noses have a poor reputation, but boxers also experience difficulties with their short noses, albeit to a lesser extent. Breathing through the nose is often audible as snorting or even snoring. The reason why boxers pant so fast is that it is easier for them to breathe through the mouth than

through the nose, which is not how it ought to be. Partly because of this, boxers are very sensitive to heat. Virtually the only way that dogs can cool down is by letting water evaporate from the mucous membrane of the mouth. Since this membrane is relatively small in relation to a boxer's body size, a boxer is affected more quickly by any rise in temperature. Consequently, physical exertion on a warm summer day is strongly advised against.

Ectropion

The lower eyelid can start to droop if the skin around the eyes is too loose, making the interior of the eyelid visible. This condition is known as ectropion and, theoretically, is a hereditary disorder. The inside of the eyelid should be pink and not red. If you see signs of weeping and red eyelids, or red conjunctival tissue in the inner corner of the eye, pay a visit to your veterinarian to have the problem assessed. Sometimes this requires surgery in order to prevent lasting damage to the eye.

12 BREEDING

A serious undertaking

If your dog or bitch has been successful at shows or competitions, or you simply have a very attractive, breed-standard boxer, the question may arise whether it is worth the trouble to use the dog for breeding. To decide this, you need to take a number of points on board. Firstly, a breeder must comply with regulations. He must be able to show that he is doing everything necessary to breed a good and, most importantly, healthy litter of boxers. In the past, demonstrable shortcomings on this point have resulted in buyers winning their cases and being compensated accordingly for damages (veterinarian fees and/or the purchase price). Consequently, both parent animals must be screened for typical hereditary disorders. Hip and elbow dysplasia come under this. You should also consider whether you ought to commence breeding with a dog whose eyelid turns outward from the eyeball (ectropion). It may only need minor surgery to correct this condition, but this does not mean that it is not better to prevent it occurring in the first place. If this is your first litter, it is a good idea to pick the brains of an experienced breeder. He or she could give you good advice and put you on the right track.

Do you have enough space?

A litter of puppies takes its toll on your home and housekee-
ping, not to mention a good night's sleep. Consider whether
you have enough space at home to house your bitch with her
pups. To begin with there must be room for the whelping
box, which in the case of a boxer should be a good five feet
wide (1.5 m). In addition, the pups will need a run where they
can play, eat, and do their business. The latter is a particularly messy job. Can you clean the area easily? A run outdoors is
also healthy for young dogs. A tiled floor is certainly easy to
keep clean, but for boisterous pups it can turn into a skating
rink and cause injuries. A grass or earth surface is better.
Finally, the little rascals produce a heap of waste in terms of
soiled newspapers if you use them to line the whelping box
and carpet the runs. It may be necessary to have this waste
removed more frequently than once every two weeks, as is
now done in many municipalities.

The cost

The costs involved are also a factor to bear in mind. Your
bitch will have to be screened in advance for HD and ED,
among other conditions. Naturally, you will have to pay the
(high) cost of these examinations even if it turns out in the end
that your bitch does not meet with requirements. The services of the future father of the pups are not for free either and
are usually comparable with the price of one puppy or slightly less. You can add the cost of gasoline to this because the
most suitable dog for your bitch seldom lives just around the
corner from you. Next, you will have to buy various items,
such as a heating lamp, whelping box, and other necessities.

Boxer pups often have relatively large heads.

Less than ideal breeders may look forward to the expansion of their bank balance, but no breeder has ever become rich from breeding dogs. Things can go badly financially. The health checks have already been mentioned, and further costs can be added for veterinary assistance during the birth and help with any of the newborn pups that are sickly. Although boxers do not suffer from difficulties in giving birth in the way that is common among bulldogs, their pups do have quite large heads, particularly if the litter is smaller in number. In practice, a smaller litter means larger pups, which means in turn an increased risk of a problem birth (possibly requiring Caesarian section). More expenditure may be necessary if you find yourself unable to attract enough interest for your pups. They then have to be vaccinated a second time, and, of course, they keep on gulping down food. A pup that is older than twelve weeks is in fact no longer a true pup because its socialization phase is then over. Finally, having your pups electronically chipped and their pedigree certification is not cheap either. Consequently, having some sort of financial buffer is really necessary.

Looking for a stud dog

The search for a suitable dog depends on a number of things, such as:

- what type of dog do you want to breed: working dogs or show dogs? Or would you be just as happy if the dog in question was simply friendly and healthy (subject to examination)?
- has the dog been used as a stud dog before, and, if so, to what extent were his good (and not so good) qualities passed on?

Cropped boxer dogs at a show

- do inherited disorders occur in his ancestry? Do not look only at the dog himself;
- can you come to satisfactory arrangements with the dog's owner about the stud fee, choice of any pup, etc.?

To deal with some of these points, you must be well informed about the ancestry of both parent animals. This is why the beginner breeder needs the assistance of someone who is better informed about these things. And even then it remains a case of trust. It also helps considerably if you attend regularly

As a rule, bitches come into heat every six months

all the various events organized by your breeders' association. This will help you develop a broader perspective on the breed.

When a bitch comes in heat (into estrus)

Most bitches come in heat (into estrus) at fairly regular intervals, usually every six months, although there can be some degree of variation in this. Give the dog's owner timely reminders about when you expect your bitch to start coming in heat. Later, call the owner when estrus starts to agree on a time for bringing the bitch over for breeding. Estrus begins with the swelling of the vulva, which is accompanied by some vaginal blood loss as well. This bleeding tails off after approximately ten days, when the bitch enters her fertile period: bitches are usually at their most fertile between the twelfth and fourteenth day and will be ready to breed. However, there are exceptions: your veterinarian can take a blood sample to determine accurately when ovulation took place.

The gestation period and afterward

The gestation period (pregnancy) in dogs lasts approximately nine weeks, or 63 to 65 days. If the bitch has become pregnant after breeding, she will usually be slightly less active than normal, although there is otherwise little else to observe. However, in the last four weeks of pregnancy, she will put on weight quickly and will also require more rest and additional food. Some breeders provide a pregnant bitch with unlimited food, always leaving the bowl full. However, it is better to

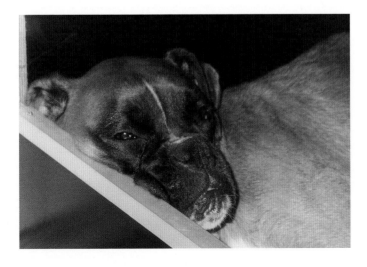

Resting on the edge of the whelping box

limit this where you have a real glutton: you must always be able to feel the ribs, even in the case of pregnant dogs. Being overweight can impede a safe delivery (whelping).

The whelping box

In the final weeks of pregnancy, place the whelping box wherever you plan to accommodate the bitch throughout the period following delivery. The box must fulfill several conditions. It must be wide enough for the bitch to lie in on her side comfortably. In practice, this is from 3 feet to 3 feet 4 inches (90 to 100 cm). The length may be one and a half times the width. This provides enough space for both mother and pups. In addition, good whelping boxes usually have a rail attached within (usually aluminum) so that the bitch cannot lie against the edge. Some bitches will sometimes squash a puppy with their backs against the edge of a box, either not hearing or properly interpreting its protesting squeaks. By fixing a rail at a height of about 4 inches (10 cm), the pup is pushed under the rail and is not squeezed between the side of the box and the mother dog (and, in the case of very young pups, killed). A heating element usually covers half the base of professional whelping boxes to keep the pups permanently warm, allowing the bitch to lie on the cooler section. As the pups get a little older, they will often seek out on their own a part of the box that suits them in terms of temperature. Ideally, the entrance to the whelping box should be closed off with a few boards or a flap to stop the pups from getting out, but allowing the bitch to do so if she wishes.

Checklist

You should have the following items at home well before whelping (delivery) begins:

- whelping box
- digital thermometer
- piles of clean towels and washcloths
- a large roll of corrugated cardboard or newspapers (to line the floor)
- puppy feeding bottle
- high-quality substitute milk
- disinfectant
- accurate digital kitchen or letter scale
- a heating lamp with red bulb
- your veterinarian's telephone number
- a notebook and pen
- scissors

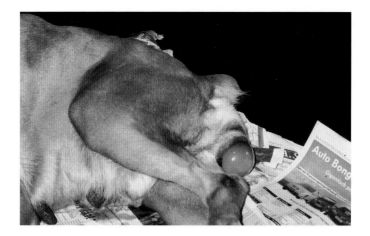

Delivery (whelping)

The bitch usually announces the onset of labor by restlessness, not wanting to eat, and having to do her business more frequently. Depending on the dog, she will either look for support or else withdraw somewhat. Sometimes, a bitch may start digging or licking herself. From a medical point of view, it is very important to make a note of the time that the first real contraction commences. You are unlikely to miss this because these contractions are quite sizable. Her flanks will convulse and there will often be a characteristic expression: she will show the whites of her eyes and often look rather helpless. The first pup should be born within an hour of the contractions starting. If this does not happen, there may be a problem that is preventing a normal birth. In that case, call the veterinarian. Generally, boxers do not have extremely difficult deliveries, but even so you must always keep your wits about you. The first thing that you will see is not usually a pup but the amniotic sac that contains it, surrounded by (a lot of) fluid. On average, if delivery goes well, you can expect something in the order of four to seven pups. Sometimes there are more, sometimes fewer. In the latter case, the pups will often be slightly larger, which can make expelling them more difficult. This also applies to pups that have died in the womb: these are often the cause of extremely difficult deliveries.

The umbilical cord

Immediately after delivery, the bitch will try to remove the sac. Boxers often need help with this because of their jaws. First of all, remove the placental sac from the pup's mouth and nose: it must now be allowed quite quickly to breathe on its own. If a

*The bitch will try
to bite through
the umbilical
cord; help is
sometimes needed*

pup breathes with a rasping noise or you see bubbles come from its nostrils, this is a sign that amniotic fluid has got into its airways. This can cause problems. You can purchase special suction pumps to remove this fluid through the nostrils and help the pup breathe normally. Afterward, the bitch will lick and bite through the umbilical cord instinctively. A short length of cord will be left attached, which must be left there at all costs. In a few days to a week it will dry out and drop off on its own. Some bitches have the urge to keep on licking and biting, which can cause wounding to the skin on the belly. Whatever you do, do not allow the bitch to keep licking. A wound to the skin is extremely hazardous if it becomes infected.

Placenta (afterbirth)

The umbilical cord is attached to the placenta. This is not necessarily delivered immediately after each pup. In any event, make a note of each placenta that is delivered. If one remains behind in the womb it can result in a life-threatening infection. Inform your veterinarian about this and he or she will will give your bitch an injection that causes the womb to contract and expel any remaining placenta or even pups. Normally, the bitch will eat any placenta. This is completely natural behavior.

After the delivery

Very young pups spend their days sleeping and drinking milk. If they are unhappy they make you well aware of it by squeaking and crawling around restlessly. Such behavior may

Pups curl up close together to keep warm.

mean that the pups are too cold or too warm, are constipated, or are not getting enough food—in other words, they are hungry. Try to get to the bottom of the cause or else ask your veterinarian to pay a visit. Pups should put on weight every day. This cannot be seen with the naked eye, which is why you should weigh the pups at around the same time each day using a scale accurate to the nearest ounce (or gram)—a letter or kitchen scales, If a puppy is not growing, it may not be getting enough milk, or there may be another problem.

Supplementary bottle feeding

Sometimes, pups need additional feeding by bottle. This might happen if your bitch has an extremely large litter and is unable to produce enough milk to feed it in proportion. It might also be that the bitch is actually producing too little milk, although this is much less common. The strongest pups usually get the best teats. You can overcome this by introducing a rotation system. Place the slightly lighter pups next to the fullest teats. Naturally, if a pup continues to lag behind in growth, you should give it an additional bottle feed. You should use a special puppy formula milk for this. Your veterinarian may not always have this in stock: make sure you already have it at home before the expected date of delivery.

Deworming
Pups should be dewormed several times before they reach eight weeks. Ask your veterinarian for a deworming preparation that is suitable for pups and follow the manufacturer's instructions.

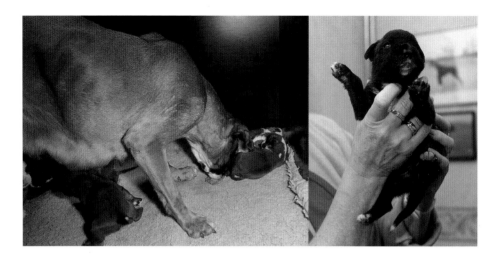

*The bitch keeps
her litter
spick-and-span*

*Just look at me
growing!*

The pups

You will not need to do much litter cleaning during the first three weeks. The mother dog will clean up tidily all the bodily waste from her offspring. You can start giving supplementary food in the fourth week. Use a weaning food that is specifically for puppies and not for human babies. Supplementary feeding changes the pups' stools and the mother will be less prepared to clean up waste or will no longer do so at all. This becomes your task from the moment you start to introduce supplementary food. Gradually expand the solid food you give so that the pups are fully weaned by the sixth week. Then try to keep them on solid food as far as possible. If you allow the bitch to remain with her offspring permanently, the pups will beleaguer her incessantly to give them just a little more milk. It is better to grant the bitch some time to rest and allow her to be with her pups at set times. Therefore, a good time to reunite the bitch with her young can be immediately after you have given the pups their meal. It is not a good idea to remove the mother dog entirely from the pups: she still retains an important function as a role model. While in this phase, try to introduce the pups to many different people, including children. This helps the pups to see humans as their "kin" and develop into confident animals. It is important to have a lot of contact with them.

The first vaccination
At seven weeks or so, pups will be drinking little or none of their mother's milk any more. Since they are no longer being protected against diseases, this is the time to commence with their first vaccination.

The new owners

The pups will be able to stand on their own feet as soon as they reach about eight weeks. The first prospective buyers might already be ringing at the door. Naturally, you will want the pups to go to good homes, which is why there is nothing wrong with being a little discerning. Ask about the space they can offer your pup, the experience that they have in bringing up a dog, and the amount of time that they can, and want, to devote to the pup. Also ask what made them want to choose a boxer pup in particular, and consider whether this fits in with your experience of the breed. If you have little faith in the prospective buyer's motivation or experience, just bide your time quietly for another buyer. There are plenty of boxer fans around. It is standard practice for the breeder to put down a few guidelines on paper as regards caring for and rearing the pup. A real purchase agreement is even worth considering. Once you have found homes at last for all the pups, your home will suddenly feel terribly quiet. You may be relieved—but, perhaps, you will miss all the commotion. If the latter sounds like you, you were probably born to be a dog breeder.

This is mine!

13 Useful addresses and photography credits

United States:

American Canine Association, Inc.
(for all addresses and general information relating to dogs)
Corporate Offices:
800 Delaware Avenue
Reg. Dept., Box 992
Wilmington DE 19899-0992
Tel: (800) 651-8332
Internet: http://www.acavet.com

American Kennel Club (A.K.C.)
5580 Centerview Drive
Raleigh NC 27606
Internet: http://www.akc.org

American Boxer Club, Inc.
Corresponding Secretary: Mrs. Barbara E. Wagner
6310 Edward Drive
Clinton MD 20735-4135
Internet: http://americanboxerclub.org

Breeder Referral Officer (for breed information and to find a breeder in your area)
Contact: Lucille Jackson
11300 Oakton Road
Oakton VA 22124-2001
Tel: (703) 385-9385

Breed Rescue Information (for older dogs)
Contact: Connie Black
8921 Camille Drive
River Ridge LA 70123
Tel: (504) 738-5820

A boxer is for life

United Kennel Club
100 East Kilgore Street
Kalamazoo MI 49001
Internet: http://www.ukcdogs.com

Canada:

Canadian Kennel Club
89 Skyway Avenue, Suite 100
Otobicoke, Ontario M9W 6R4
Tel: 415-675 5511
Internet: http://www.ckc.ca

Boxer Club of Canada Inc.
Membership Secretary: Mary Dulong
678 MacLaren Drive
Burlington, Ontario L7N 2Z2
Internet: http://boxerclubofcanada.com

Photography credits
All of the photographs were taken by the author with the
exception of:
Toon Hendrix: pages 7, 48 above, 56, 90, 93, 113, 124 right
and 127
Bert Jansen: pages 119, 121 and 122
Esther Verhoef/Furry Tails: pages 13, 15, 37, 103, 107, 115
and 118
Ivon de Vet: pages 18, 108 and 125 above
Photographs on pages 6 and 10 are from the book
Hondenrassen from Graaf van Bylandt (1900)